THE ART OF SIMPLE LIVING

An Hachette UK Company
www.hachette.co.uk

Vie Books, an imprint of Summersdale Publishers Ltd
Part of Octopus Publishing Group Limited
Carmelite House
50 Victoria Embankment
LONDON
EC4Y 0DZ
UK

www.summersdale.com

Printed and bound in China

ISBN: 978-1-78783-999-1

Substantial discounts on bulk quantities of Summersdale books are available to corporations, professional associations and other organizations. For details contact general enquiries: telephone: +44 (0)1243 771107 or email: enquiries@summersdale.com.

- THE ART OF -
SIMPLE
LIVING

Practical Steps to Slowing Down, Finding
Peace and Enjoying a Wholesome Life

SAM LACEY

CONTENTS

INTRODUCTION

Modern-day living is fabulous in so many ways: we have access to so much more than our parents and grandparents – but therein lies the problem. Our lives have become so full of "stuff" – noise, clutter, pop-up ads, technology, media, opinions, stress – that often it can be hard to see the wood for the trees. Not only that, but we overfill our diaries with appointments, evenings out and coffee catch-ups with friends, leaving little time for our own self-care. The good news is that we can leave the chaos behind and achieve inner peace and happiness by taking some simple steps to a more relaxed, cheaper and sustainable way of life. Picking up this book is just the start. Throughout its five chapters you'll find a wealth of help, advice and tips on how to achieve a simpler and stress-free existence. Would you like answers to questions like: How can I turn down social invitations I'm not interested in? Where do I even begin with decluttering my home? What kinds of activities can I do that won't break the bank? How can I get healthy meals on the table without spending a fortune on ingredients and hours in the kitchen? What makes an ideal staycation? "Yes, please!" we hear you cry. Then dive on in.

PART 1:
IN THE HOME

Home is where the heart is – it's also where we spend a lot of our time, whether at work or at play – so it is the ideal place to begin your simple-living journey. There are many things you can do to achieve peace and relaxation throughout your space: some are quick and easy to achieve; others will need a bit more planning and can be tackled when you have more time on your hands. Start with small tasks, then when you realize how these little things can start to make a difference, you can expand your happy-home horizons!

MAKE THE MOST OF IT

Comparing your home to other people's will not bring you joy. Late-night scrolling through Instagram looking at images of "perfect" homes aside, it can be really tempting to sit and look around your house or flat and think you need to move to gain more light and space. In fact, it may not be lack of light and space that's the issue; it could just be that you need to think about what you do have in a different way. For instance, the colours you use throughout your home will affect the feel of it; darker or duller hues will bring walls in, so painting them in pale, neutral shades is a simple and cost-effective way to reflect light and make a room feel larger. That said, if you can't be without colour then you could add a bit of pizzazz with just one feature wall or a bright pair of curtains. The following few pages contain some tips and ideas for some of the rooms in your home, to both create the impression of more space and breathe in some new life. When you're done, you won't want to leave.

Living room

- How many people use the living room at the same time on a day-to-day basis? Perhaps you only need enough permanent seating for that many. Utilize multifunctional furniture, like ottomans with lift-up tops, for extra seating and storage. On the occasions you have visitors, bring out a fold-out chair or beanbag for additional seats.

- An effective way to "add height" to a room is to install simple floor-to-ceiling shelving to draw your eyes up. Try not to overload the shelves though – just display special pieces or items that you love, rather than stuffing them full of clutter!

- To brighten a dark corner, hang a large wall mirror or a light-coloured photograph or picture; add a tall floor lamp for some soft evening lighting.

Kitchen

- Simply clearing the work surfaces of any utensils and equipment at the end of each day equals instant space, whatever size kitchen you have. If you have enough drawers, store equipment in them rather than in pots on the work surface and stow away washing-up brushes and cloths under the sink. And, of course, everyone has that end-of-worktop area where a pile of junk mail and bills accumulates; aim to spend a few minutes each day dealing with it instead of letting it sit there gathering dust and crumbs. To avoid bills gathering on work surfaces at all, you could change to paperless billing.

- If your kitchen-cupboard doors are boring and gloomy, consider giving them a facelift by painting them in a light or vibrant shade. There are some excellent paints available now, which have been specially designed for this very purpose – it's a much cheaper option than a whole new refit and you'll gain the satisfaction of having achieved it yourself.

◆ Most of us don't use gadgets like the bread-maker, food mixer or ice-cream maker every day, so put them away in a cupboard. And if you don't use them at all, either sell them on or gift them to a friend or family member who will use them.

Bedroom

Bedrooms should be a haven of relaxation and calm, so clear surfaces and bedside tables of anything that you don't need immediately to hand. Use under-bed storage boxes to stow away any throws, cushions and blankets when they're not in use; adding sachets of fresh lavender will help to keep away moths. Hanging window dressings in the same colour as the walls can also give the impression of more space. And remember to put your clothes in the laundry or hang them in the wardrobe before you turn in for the night.

Bathroom

Invest in a wall-mounted shower or bath caddy to organize your bottles of shampoo and shower gel, so they don't start to gather on surfaces. Better still, shampoo bars last way longer, take up less room and are much better for the environment. Install storage or shelving above the toilet, as this is great usable space.

GIVE SOMETHING A NEW LEASE OF LIFE

It may bring a rush of excitement when you buy something new, but how long does that feeling actually last? And when it wears off it's more than likely you'll head out and buy something else. That's not to say you can't ever treat yourself to new things, but investing in second-hand items can be just as rewarding – plus, you've got something a bit different that nobody else owns. Charity shops, car boot sales, garage sales and online auction sites are a treasure trove of unloved items where you can pick things up for a fraction of the price of something new, including clothing, shoes and household items. Spend a rainy weekend giving an old chest of drawers a lick of paint and some new handles and you've got an individual piece that you've put the hard work into to enjoy.

Upcycling 101

Here are a few ideas for some fun weekend upcycling projects for beginners; loads more inspiration can be found in online blogs by upcycling enthusiasts!

* Empty tin cans make great candleholders or colourful pots. Wash them in hot, soapy water, let them dry and file down any rough edges around the top, taking care as they will be sharp. For candleholders, drill or punch small holes in the sides and pop in a tea light, or make an attractive penholder or plant pot for home-grown herbs by sticking wrapping paper or winding rope around the outside.

* An unloved, framed mirror can be repurposed as a beautiful candle tray. Paint the frame in a colour of your choosing, and place four or five candles on it to reflect soft light around a room.

* Brighten up wooden pallets by painting them, then use them for all manner of things: in the garden to store bits and pieces, flip them on their side and use them for books or turn one upside down as a rustic coffee table.

♦ If you have retro band T-shirts hidden away in drawers, create some memory artwork with them. Pick up an old frame from a charity shop and display either the whole shirt, or cut out the image and the tour dates and frame them.

LOOK FOR SUSTAINABLE ALTERNATIVES

Ten household items you should avoid buying

1. Paper kitchen towel – often only used to wipe up the odd spill.

2. Plastic toothbrushes – commonly found in beach clean-ups.

3. Fast fashion – cheap clothing that isn't made to last.

4. Plastic food wrap and foil – neither are usually recyclable.

5. Bottled water – an expensive option that creates excess landfill.

6. Plastic straws – bad for the environment and for wildlife.

7. Cotton pads – these don't biodegrade due to the bleaching and mixing process.

8. Plastic bin bags – may be made to measure your particular brand of bin, but often aren't biodegradable and are more expensive.

9. Ornaments and knick-knacks – not only do these create clutter on surfaces, but they are something else to dust!

10. Single-use batteries.

... and ten eco-friendly replacements

1 Reusable bamboo kitchen towels – look on marketplace sites like Etsy for this eco-friendly alternative to paper kitchen towels.

2 Bamboo toothbrushes – highly sustainable, safe and eco-friendly.

3 Second-hand or home-made clothing – hit the charity shops or teach yourself to sew.

4 Beeswax food wraps (reusable), paper food bags (recyclable) or stainless-steel lunch boxes.

5 Filtered tap water.

6 Paper straws can be recycled and you can buy metal reusable straws (or just drink from the glass!).

7 Reusable cotton pads – washable.

8 Biodegradable bin bags – now come in a wide range of shapes and sizes.

9 Houseplants or framed photographs of your own memories – this makes a lovely alternative craft project, too.

10 Rechargeable batteries – possibly a little more of an outlay in the short term, but much more economical in the long run.

STOP BUYING, START (MINIMAL) LIVING

If you've ever moved home, it can be a real eye-opener to find out just how much you accumulate without realizing. Try this: go to any room in your home and take a good, honest look around at all the stuff. Do you use it all? If some of it was gone, would you miss it? The way in which we live these days is often fuelled by a desire to fill our lives with things to "keep up" with other people, their homes, their clothes, their shiny electronics – isn't that exhausting? The fact is, this often means owning a lot of things that we don't need, and which won't bring us long-term satisfaction. And it's not just material items. Our tendencies toward overconsumption extend to food, energy and resources – all of this can be minimized and simplified, helping to give our brains, and our homes, room to breathe. If enough of us make changes, the knock-on effect for our own mental health – as well as the planet and our future as human beings – could be huge. Minimalism isn't just about owning less, but also about making space for what matters more. It is about finding the solution for you, personally, between the things that make you happy, and freeing yourself of the things that don't. With fewer

"things" to distract you, you'll feel less mentally drained and have more time and energy to focus on yourself, your friends and your family – all of which are more important. If this sounds good, the following few sections will offer some tips for aspiring minimalists to get started, including how to control your spending and the art of decluttering and creating your calm.

HOW DO I STOP BUYING STUFF?

First of all, it's important to realize why you are spending money on superfluous stuff before you try and curb the habit. And it is often just that: a habit. We tend to buy things for ourselves and our home because we are bored, or to make ourselves feel better after a bad day – or to celebrate a good one. In the case of food, we can make irrational or expensive purchases when we're hungry or tempted by promotional offers. Every time you go to buy something, ask yourself: do I actually *need* it? To set you off on the road to minimal spending, the next page shows a couple of ways to help you cut down.

Option 1: Try going cold turkey and make a pledge to not spend any money – apart from on food or bills – for one month. Any time you feel the urge to splash out on something, don't; put the money in a savings account instead. At the end of the month see how much you would have spent on things you have managed to do without. Can you do the same the following month, and the next? You could put the money you save toward a longer-term goal like a holiday or a new car.

Option 2: Cut down gradually. Try one month without takeaway coffee, the following month not eating out, the next without buying clothes... you get the idea. Each month that you go without buying something, the more you'll realize you can do without it. Either save the cash instead or make a donation to a charity you support.

BUDGETING

A straightforward way to keep track of where your cash goes is to keep a record. You can easily do this yourself using a simple spreadsheet, logging your daily spend.

At the start of each month, in the first column list all of your regular "money in" (e.g. salary) and all regular outgoings in the second column (e.g. mortgage/rent, electricity, mobile phone); be honest about these. Every time you buy something, it goes into the spreadsheet. Use column three to keep a running total using a simple formula ($C = A - B$). By knocking off regular outgoings from your balance up front, you know exactly what you'll have left. And if you're not tech-savvy, then don't worry – you can budget just as well with a notebook, a pen and a calculator.

Why do I need to track my spending?

So, why do this? Isn't the idea to live a simpler life, rather than add to it? Actually, tracking your spending makes the decision about whether to buy those new shoes, or how much you can save, pretty cut and dried – with the ultimate goal of worry-free, organized, simple finances. There are also plenty of brilliant free apps that will help you to manage your finances, like Mint, YNAB or PocketGuard, which can alert you to overspending and help you to save.

Quick budgeting tips

◆ Use spare cash to pay off any credit cards before you save – you'll likely pay more interest on a credit- or store-card bill than you'll earn on savings. Look for 0 per cent transfer offers for credit-card balances to cut the interest.

◆ Put any spare loose change in a jar and when it's full, count it up and save it.

◆ Always review any regular bills annually – such as those for energy and car insurance – rather than letting them roll over. There are lots of websites to help you do this.

◆ Cancel any subscriptions that you haven't used for three months.

◆ Consider having a smart meter fitted to monitor your energy use – or use a power-meter plug so you can see which appliances in your home use the most energy.

DECLUTTERING

So now you're on the road to buying less stuff, let's think about how to remove some of the things that you don't need, to pave the way for your minimal home. The main rule for decluttering is to start with things that you don't have any sentimental attachment to. There are several ways of going about decluttering: let's look at these in turn.

One room at a time

One of the easiest rooms to declutter is the bathroom, so start with this first. Then move on to your bedroom, saving the larger areas like the kitchen, living room or home office until last – when you're in the swing of it. Take three boxes with you into each room: one for recycling/ repurposing (e.g. empty bottles or things that could be upcycled), one for rehoming/selling (e.g. unopened items that you won't use, clothes you don't wear) and one for rubbish.

By category

Ideas for categories include: clothes/shoes (see page 32 for more detail on clearing out clothing and creating a capsule wardrobe); jewellery; books; electronics; crockery; toiletries; children's

toys; stationery; cleaning supplies. Leave sentimental items until last as dealing with these is not easy. If you really can't let something go just yet, don't let it take up space in a drawer: wear your grandad's old jumper around the house; take photos of your children's artwork and save them in a digital album; create a memory box for smaller keepsakes. Enlisting an honest opinion from a friend on what to keep can also help.

Smaller chunks

To avoid "decluttering apathy", do it in stages. It doesn't matter if you don't clear out your whole home in one weekend; the point is that you're making a start and every step – no matter how small – is progress.

IDEAS FOR REHOMING YOUR STUFF

- **Donate to charity or a shelter** – as well as charity shops, think about other places in need. Children's toys could go to a local preschool or nursery, clothing could be really welcomed at a homeless shelter or a refuge. Old towels and sheets, as well as spare pet supplies and excess food, are usually gratefully received by animal shelters and rehoming centres.

- **Food banks** – these accept non-perishable food, as well as other essential items like household, baby-care and hygiene products.

- **Gift to a friend or relative** – there's no need to offload your old junk on to people just because you don't want it anymore, but if it's something that's genuinely lovely that you just don't need, then by all means pass it on.

- **Sell it on** – there are tons of places where you can make cash from unwanted possessions – eBay, Vinted, Facebook selling groups, Amazon marketplace, neighbourhood groups, Craigslist, to name just a few.

"UNDER 30-MINUTE" DECLUTTERING TASKS

Not much time? Don't worry – you can still make a start!

Kitchen

Throw away out-of-date food from kitchen cupboards and the fridge. Match plastic containers with their lids; either recycle the odd ones or keep them in a separate place as spares. Rehome recipe books that you haven't used in the past year.

Bathroom

Root out expired medication and return to a pharmacy; medicines should not be thrown in the bin or put down the sink. Go through your towels. Any with holes and stains could be donated to an animal shelter (see opposite).

Living room

Sort through your DVDs. Do you watch them? If not, rehome them or sell them online.

Bedroom

Sort through your sock drawer and throw out odd socks or those with holes in, and discard any underwear that has seen better days!

NO-TV NIGHTS

Part of living a simpler life is going back to basics in terms of how we spend our time. Previous generations didn't zap their dinner in the microwave and plonk themselves in front of the TV every night, so why do we?

Crosswords and cryptic crosswords improve your vocabulary and logical thinking; sudoku gets your maths brain whirring!

Why not teach yourself some card games? *Chase the Queen* or *Go Fish* are simple to learn and fun to play. Or have a solo game of *Clock Patience*. Learn how to play these games and lots of others on YouTube.

An oldie but a goodie: read a book. If you've always enjoyed fiction then try an autobiography. If you're a non-fiction fan, then try a well-known classic novel. Mix it up a bit!

Crafts like cross-stitch, knitting and sewing unlock your creativity – and you'll have something to show for it, like a piece of home-made artwork or something individual to wear. There are loads of YouTube tutorials on teaching yourself to knit and sew.

Listen to a podcast on your phone – from comedy and film reviews, to sport and pop culture, there are hundreds to pick from. Maybe have a go at a jigsaw while you listen.

Scrapbooking isn't just for kids. If your decluttering has turned up concert tickets, postcards and old photos that you can't live without, then organize them into scrapbooks that you can enjoy at your leisure.

On a clear evening, lie on a blanket outside and gaze up at the stars. There are some great apps that can help you track the constellations. You might just catch sight of a shooting star.

BECOME A GARDENING GURU

Spending time in nature is humbling, so try creating your own green space where you can switch off, de-stress and feel more grounded. You don't need a garden with acres of lush green lawn; you can make the most of a small patio or even just a balcony. And if you don't have any outside space, you can bring the wonders of nature inside. Here are a few tips and ideas for novice gardeners.

Planting

If you do have a garden, then the direction in which it faces will dictate to an extent the plants that will grow in it. Make a note of where the sun lands throughout the day and the evening, and start researching plants that will grow in those areas. You don't need to become a plant expert to create a beautiful space; you can ask advice from a green-fingered friend or scatter pollinator-friendly wildflower seeds and let them grow as nature intended.

Welcome in wildlife

Install a bug hotel and hang bird feeders to encourage insects and feathered friends into your space. Look online for inspiration on what kind of eco-friendly materials you can use or recycle.

Add a personal touch

A great way to add a new lease of life to a plain patio area is to use stencils and eco-friendly outdoor paint – or if you're arty, get creative with your own freehand designs. Upcycle old colanders to make hanging baskets with ready-made drainage holes and use an old bookshelf to store pots and watering cans.

Keep houseplants

If you don't have a garden, bring the outside into your home by looking after houseplants. From high-maintenance orchids and bonsai trees, to easy-to-care-for succulents, there are plenty to choose from depending on how involved you want to be. Houseplants will also instil a feeling of peace in a home-working space.

SCALE DOWN YOUR WARDROBE

Wouldn't the decision about what to put on each morning be much simpler if there was less to choose from? The theory behind a capsule wardrobe is to have a set of timeless items that can be mixed and matched to make several outfits that you love and in which you feel confident and well put together. Here are five steps to wardrobe simplicity.

Step 1

First of all, evaluate what's essential. If you work at home and attend very few meetings, then you're unlikely to need many smart pieces. And if you rarely go clubbing these days, then those sparkly platforms might need to go.

Step 2

Create a checklist for items that you have decided you need in your capsule wardrobe and determine how much of each type of clothing you're going to keep. The idea is that you can mix and match easily so bear this in mind as you're creating your list.

Step 3

Separate your checklist into smart/casual and then into categories, for example: shoes/boots; trousers/shorts; skirts/dresses; tops; accessories and bags; outerwear.

Step 4

Look at what you have. Pull out and keep anything that fits with your list. Assess what's left and either sell, donate or rehome it. There are some tips on what to do with your stuff on page 26.

Step 5

Going forward, only buy something if it mixes and matches with your wardrobe – and try to buy things that will last, rather than opting for fast fashion. Sticking to the same brand, or knowing what size you take in a certain store, will also make shopping trips much less time-consuming.

SCANDINAVIAN MINIMALISM

To round off all the points discussed in this chapter, we can all take a few lessons in simple living from Sweden by practising the philosophy of *lagom*, which means "just the right amount" or "in moderation", to achieve balance and contentment in our lives. For example, your home is *lagom* when it has neither too little nor too much in it – in other words, it's about striking a balance between bare minimalism and too much clutter. Living in this way allows you to be creative and focus on other areas of your life, so this is where decluttering, talked about earlier in this chapter, comes into play. Swedish people also practise *lagom* as it's better for the environment; if you only have what you need, you are going to save valuable natural resources as well as money. As well as within the home, the Scandinavian approach can be applied to other areas of your life such as your relationships and your food, both of which are covered in other chapters of this book. As with all elements of a simple home, deciding whether something is too much, too little, or *lagom* will vary widely from person to person; do what feels right for you.

PART 2:
MEALTIMES

Cooking simple, delicious meals yourself doesn't have to be complicated or expensive. It's also much healthier to make your own food as you know exactly what's gone into it. In this section you'll find ideas and inspiration for things like nutritious dinners on a budget, seasonal cooking and mindful eating. You'll also find information about making good food choices – when eating in and dining out – along with some simple recipes for easy home-cooked meals that can be prepared with minimum fuss.

SIMPLE PRAWN AND PEA SPAGHETTI (Serves 4)

To kick off this section, here's a quick and simple weekday recipe that can be ready in under half an hour, from prep to plate. Perfect after a long day.

Ingredients

320 g (11 oz) dried spaghetti

1 tbsp vegetable oil

1 tbsp butter

2 cloves garlic, peeled and finely chopped

650 g (1 lb 7 oz) cherry tomatoes, halved

300 g (10½ oz) raw king prawns, spines removed and cleaned

100 g (3½ oz) frozen peas, cooked and drained

dash lemon juice

fresh basil leaves

handful grated Parmesan cheese

salt and pepper

Method

Bring a large saucepan of water to the boil, then add the spaghetti. Cook according to the packet instructions – usually around 10–11 minutes.

Heat the vegetable oil and butter together in a frying pan on a medium heat. Add the garlic and fry for a few minutes until lightly browned.

Add the cherry tomatoes to the pan, seeds down. Squash them a little to release some of the juice and cook for a few minutes.

Add the prawns and heat through until pink and completely cooked through.

Finally, add the peas and cook for 2 minutes.

Add a dash of lemon juice, then serve the mixture on top of the cooked, drained spaghetti. Season to taste and garnish with the basil leaves and grated Parmesan cheese.

SLOW DOWN YOUR COOKING

If you own a slow cooker but haven't used it in ages, now's the time to dust it off. They are excellent time-savers as you can batch-cook several portions in one go and pop them in the freezer for those days when you don't have the time or the inclination to cook – and cheaper, less tender cuts of meat are ideal for slow cooking on the "low" setting to bring out their best. Slow cooking is also just as splendid for vegetarian and vegan dishes. All the recipes in this section are suitable for a larger, "family-sized" slow cooker.

VEGAN DHAL (Serves 4)

Ingredients

2 red onions, diced

4 cloves garlic, crushed

1 small to medium (approx. 850 g) butternut squash, peeled and cut into 1.5 cm (½ in.) cubes

300 g (10½ oz) dried lentils

400 ml (13½ fl oz) tin coconut milk

400 g (14 oz) tin chopped tomatoes

turmeric, mild curry powder and chilli powder (add to taste, depending on how spicy you like it)

handful fresh spinach leaves

salt and pepper

Method

Put everything apart from the spinach in the slow cooker, give it a stir and cook on "low" for 6–8 hours or "high" for 4–5 hours.

Just before serving, stir in the fresh spinach and season to taste. Serve with rice.

EASY-PEASY MACARONI CHEESE (Serves 6)

Ingredients

400 g (14 oz) dried macaroni or rigatoni pasta

200 g (7 oz) Cheddar cheese

200 g (7 oz) grated mozzarella cheese

cheese sauce (see right)

salt and pepper

For the cheese sauce

45 g (1½ oz) butter

45 g (1½ oz) flour

570 ml (19 fl oz) milk

100 g (3½ oz) grated hard cheese

Method

Make your cheese sauce. Melt the butter and stir in the flour, cooking for a minute or two over a low heat. Gradually add the milk, a little at a time, making sure the flour is absorbed each time. Once all the milk is added, bring to the boil and simmer for 5–6 minutes until the sauce has thickened. Stir in the cheese and let it melt.

Place the pasta, Cheddar and mozzarella in the pot. Pour over the cheese sauce and season with salt and pepper.

Cook on "high" for 2 hours, stirring 30 minutes before the end of the cooking time; be careful not to overcook as the pasta will be too soft.

Season to taste and serve with garlic bread on the side.

CHEAP AND CHEERFUL RICE PUDDING
(Serves 6)

Ingredients

250 g (9 oz) pudding rice

2.5 litres (4 ½ pt) semi-skimmed milk

6 tbsp golden caster sugar

1½ tsp unsalted butter

1½ tsp vanilla extract

Method

Put all of the ingredients in the pot, pop the lid on and cook on "high" for 3 hours. Give it a stir a few times while it's cooking. Eat it warm (let it cool for 5 minutes as it will be super-hot when it's cooked) or enjoy it cold the next day.

INDULGENT FRUIT CAKE
(Serves 12)

Ingredients

800 g (1 lb 12 oz)
mixed dried fruit

750 ml (1 ⅓ pt)
semi-skimmed milk

250 g (9 oz) self-
raising flour

200 g (7 oz) mixed nuts

Method

Soak the fruit overnight in the milk. If you're feeling adventurous, swap out 100 ml (3½ fl oz) of the milk for 100 ml (3½ fl oz) brandy.

Completely line your slow cooker with thick baking paper.

Gently combine the flour and the nuts with the fruit and place the cake mix in the pot.

Lay a clean tea towel over the top, then place the lid on. Cook on "low" for around 8 hours.

Lift it out of the pot using the baking paper and leave to cool, or eat warm with lots of custard!

GO NATURAL

We all know that we shouldn't eat too much processed food. As well as costing us more and often being encased in excess packaging, it's usually full of hidden nasties and refined sugar which, if we overload on, can lead to weight gain and associated health problems. Of course, banning biscuits forever may not be realistic – the odd treat won't hurt – but when making dietary choices, bear in mind that your body needs to work harder to digest junk food, which can make you tired and lethargic. One of the best approaches to simple eating, which ensures you get enough vitamins and minerals, is to follow a natural diet and eat "real food". For example, items such as fruit, vegetables, meat, crops or nuts and seeds – basically things that look like food! If you're in any doubt about a product, then have a quick read of the ingredients list; if it's as long as your arm and full of numbers, then perhaps you should rethink the purchase.

Feeling fruity?

Isn't fruit marvellous? As well as tasting amazing, it ticks the simple eating box by being completely natural. As an added bonus, many fruits have some hidden talents…

- Bananas contain vitamin B6, magnesium, potassium and tryptophan. These work in combination to relax muscles and make melatonin, both of which are conducive to a restful night.

- Pineapples contain a substance called bromelain, which acts as an anti-inflammatory. In fact, some studies have shown bromelain may have the potential to protect against cancer.

- Apples contain pectin, a prebiotic that helps with digestion and metabolism.

- Pomegranates have three times as many antioxidants as green tea.

- While strawberries taste really sweet, they have quite a low glycaemic index so won't cause a blood-sugar spike.

- As well as being high in fibre and vitamins C and K, blueberries are known for their powerful antioxidant properties and may reduce the risk of conditions such as heart disease and diabetes.

SUSTAINABLE EATING

What we put into our bodies doesn't just affect our health, it affects the health of our planet, too. According to Greenpeace, to prevent climate breakdown we need to cut our dairy and meat consumption by 70 per cent. Currently, 26 per cent of the land on Earth is used for grazing livestock and with demand for meat on the increase this simply isn't sustainable, leading to deforestation and knock-on effects for other species. If you're a committed carnivore, perhaps you could start by having one or two "meat-free" evenings during the week? Could you also consume less dairy? Food for thought.

Should I stop eating meat altogether?

Changing your way of eating is a personal decision, however, if you are thinking about becoming vegetarian or opting for a solely plant-based diet, here are some things to consider.

- Vegetarians and vegans are likely to eat even more than the recommended five a day; as we know, fruit and vegetables have a multitude of health benefits.

- Non-meat diets are also full of high-protein legumes – the consumption of which are linked to lower incidences of heart disease.

- Plant-based foods are rich in phytonutrients, which protect against age-related diseases.

- A vegan diet may help you to lose weight.

Do remember that it isn't just a case of eating what you normally do and simply cutting out meat and fish (vegetarian) or all animal products (vegan). Your diet should be planned properly so you replace the vitamins and nutrients that animal-based diets provide. If you're in any doubt at all, then speak to your doctor.

THAI SWEET POTATO CURRY (Serves 6)

Nutritious, warming and vegan. What's not to love? You could make a double quantity and freeze in individual portions.

Ingredients

1 tbsp vegetable oil

1 red onion, chopped

1 yellow pepper, chopped

2 cloves garlic, chopped

3 large sweet potatoes, peeled and cut into 1.5 cm (½ in.) chunks

2 tsp Thai red curry paste

400 ml (13½ fl oz) coconut milk

200 g (7 oz) tin chickpeas, rinsed and drained

handful fresh spinach, chopped

salt and pepper

Method

Heat the vegetable oil in a large pan, then fry the onion, pepper and garlic for 5 minutes, until soft. Add the sweet potato, curry paste and coconut milk and bring to the boil then reduce to a medium heat for 10–12 minutes, stirring occasionally.

Add the rinsed and drained chickpeas and cook for a further 5 minutes.

Season to taste and serve with brown rice, a squeeze of lime and warm naan bread.

EAT CLOSE
TO HOME

Another simple way to become more sustainable in your food choices is to think about where it has actually come from. How many miles has it travelled, for example, by the time it ends up in your shopping basket? Think about supporting local producers by shopping at venues like farmers' markets and smaller shops. If you do shop at the supermarket, then choose fresh vegetables and fruit that's in season, rather than varieties that have been "forced", stored for months, or travelled thousands of miles in a plane. Eating seasonally will also mean the food tastes better and will be less expensive; as you're buying foods that are in more plentiful supply, it costs less to get it from the field to the shop. Making these kinds of changes to the way you eat has the added benefit of keeping money in the local economy: a win–win.

Growing your own

The ultimate way to really know where your food has come from is to grow it yourself. Plus, it's really satisfying to know that you're enjoying the fruits of your own labour. Start small by either sectioning off a small piece of back garden, or grow things like runner beans or potatoes in pots and containers, or tomato plants in grow-bags. Once you really get the hang of it, you could think about an allotment space.

What and when?

Fruit and vegetables are a good first choice for novice home-farmers, as well as herbs like mint, basil or chives, which you can grow either in a garden, or in containers on a windowsill. Leafy greens and vegetables should be planted just before the summer. In a moderate climate, fruits should be planted in early spring; fruit trees can be grown in containers through the summer, but should then be protected from frost over the winter. Potatoes and other "underground" vegetables like beetroot and turnips like to grow through the colder months. If you've never grown your own food before, ask advice from a green-fingered friend or family member, or chat to someone at a local garden centre.

A QUICK GUIDE TO (SOME) SEASONAL FOOD

This quick reference shows just a tiny selection of the fruits and vegetables that are in season throughout the world – there are many more to choose from!

March–April

Northern hemisphere: lemons, limes, pineapples, rhubarb, asparagus, sweet potatoes, kale, leeks

Southern hemisphere: blackberries, cumquats, guavas, grapes, pawpaw, artichokes, beetroot, pak choi

---

May–September

Northern hemisphere: apricots, blueberries, cherries, gooseberries, strawberries, artichokes, cucumbers, green beans, mushrooms

Southern hemisphere: custard apples, mandarins, persimmons, watermelons, artichokes, celery, aubergines

October–November

Northern hemisphere: blackberries, apples, cranberries, figs, pears, kiwi fruit, pomegranates, beetroot, broccoli, peppers, Brussels sprouts, carrots, cauliflower, celeriac

Southern hemisphere: avocados, bananas, papaya, passion fruit, pineapples, mangoes, limes, lychees, artichokes, asparagus, beetroot, broccoli, cabbage

---

December–February

Northern hemisphere: oranges, persimmons, kiwi fruit, beetroot, chicory, turnips, horseradish

Southern hemisphere: cherries, loganberries, Valencia oranges, pineapples, peas, radishes, tomatoes, squash

SATISFYING HOME-MADE VEGETABLE SOUP (Serves 6)

Once you have harvested your first veggie crop, try this simple soup recipe to bring out their best.

Ingredients

1 tbsp vegetable oil

1 large onion, chopped

2 cloves garlic, chopped

1 tbsp smoked paprika

1 tbsp dried mixed herbs

1 tsp each salt and black pepper

3 large potatoes, chopped into 2.5 cm (1 in.) chunks

600 g (1 lb 5 oz) other home-grown vegetables such as carrots, sweetcorn, squash, peppers, celery, broccoli, courgettes, chopped into 2.5 cm (1 in.) chunks

2 x 400 g (14 oz) tins chopped tomatoes

500 ml (17½ fl oz) vegetable stock

crème fraîche (to serve)

salt and pepper

Method

In a large casserole pot, heat the oil and lightly fry the onion and garlic until soft. Then add the paprika, mixed herbs, salt and pepper, and stir through.

Add the potatoes and all the vegetables to the pot. Stir well then add the tinned tomatoes and the stock. Bring to the boil, then simmer for 30 minutes until the vegetables have all softened.

Season to taste and spoon into bowls. Add a generous dollop of crème fraîche and serve with crusty bread.

WASTE NOT, WANT NOT

We've all thrown away bendy carrots and mouldy courgettes that we've found lurking in the bottom of the fridge – but did you know that roughly one third of all the food produced globally is either discarded (i.e. by shops when it's not sold to consumers), lost (spoiled during distribution) or thrown away? Most of us are really lucky to have a wide choice and abundance of food, but this means we can buy or cook more than we need, and then often think nothing of throwing it out if we don't use it. Now think about the 800 million or so fellow humans who don't have access to affordable or nutritious food. Food waste that rots in landfills also produces methane, which contributes to greenhouse gases. So, how can we reduce our food waste?

- If you shop regularly at the same place, ask when they usually reduce their stock. Buying items that shops are likely to have to throw out means they'll have less food wastage, too.

- Unless it's a staple item that you will use, be wary of deals. They can make you think you're getting a bargain, when you might not need or use the extra amount and it could end up as landfill.

- Take stock of what's in your fridge every few days; if something is about to expire, then try and incorporate it into a meal – or offer it to a neighbour!

- Non-perishable items like tinned food, pasta and cereals can be donated to food banks. Someone will be really happy to receive something you don't need.

- Vegetables that have lost their appeal could be added to a compost bin and broken down to use in the garden.

ADD NEW LIFE
TO LEFTOVERS

Rather than bin leftover food, you can often turn it into another meal by adding a few extra store-cupboard ingredients. Below is a recipe for using up leftover chicken from a roast.

ROAST-CHICKEN PASTA (Serves 4)

Ingredients

300 g (10½ oz) pasta, any type

1 tbsp butter or vegetable oil

1 onion, chopped

1 clove garlic, chopped

a few rashers lean bacon, chopped

couple handfuls leftover meat from a roast chicken, chopped

200 ml (7 fl oz) vegetable stock

1 tbsp wholegrain or Dijon mustard

handful peas

3 tbsp crème fraîche

salt and pepper

Method

Boil some water and cook the pasta. Meanwhile, heat the butter or vegetable oil in a sauté pan on a medium heat, then add the onion and garlic until they soften.

Add the bacon and cook until crisp, then add the roast chicken and heat through.

Add the vegetable stock and mustard and simmer for 10 minutes, dropping in the peas for the final 2 minutes.

Reduce the heat and stir through the crème fraîche. Season to taste and serve in warmed pasta bowls.

MONEY-SAVING MENU TIPS

With a bit of planning, and knowing what to look out for, it is possible to reduce the amount you spend on the weekly shop.

♦ Meal-plan your week. Not only will this tell you exactly what you need to buy and how much (also meaning less waste), it'll take the hassle out of deciding what to have for dinner.

♦ Buy reduced fresh produce that's reached its sell-by date and freeze it to make it last longer.

♦ Cheaper, store-own brands in less fussy packets are often just as good as popular branded goods.

♦ As well as what you buy, think about where you buy it. Potatoes are potatoes, whether you buy them in the expensive supermarket or the budget one.

♦ Odd-shaped vegetables are often reduced – they taste exactly the same!

- Look in "reduced" baskets at the end of aisles for items in dented tins or squashed packets; again, this won't affect the quality of the food itself.

- Don't buy prepared food like grated cheese or chopped vegetables. It may save 5 minutes in the kitchen but it's much more expensive.

- Buy extra-large packs of things like toilet rolls, washing powder and dishwasher tablets if you have the space to store them, as they usually work out cheaper.

- Look on the lower shelves for better deals; shops often place the things *they* want you to buy at eye-level, but this isn't always the most economical option.

- Try shopping on a full stomach to avoid snacks "accidentally" falling into your basket!

- If you can, go shopping without your kids; taking them with you can mean lots of extras may end up in the trolley for a quiet life!

ONE-DISH FISH PIE (Serves 4)

One-pot meals are a great time-saver – with the added bonus of not much washing-up. (OK, so this also needs two saucepans to cook the potato and make a cheese sauce, but still meets minimum washing-up requirements!)

Ingredients

For the pie

1 kg (2 lb 4 oz) potatoes, peeled and halved

100 g (3½ oz) butter

240 g (8½ oz) skinless, boneless smoked haddock fillets

240 g (8½ oz) skinless, boneless salmon fillets

150 g (5 oz) cooked king prawns

500 g (1 lb 2 oz) leeks, trimmed, halved lengthwise, sliced crosswise 2.5 cm (1 in.) thick and washed

100 g (3½ oz) fresh spinach, washed

cheese sauce (see below)

100 g (3½ oz) grated cheese

For the cheese sauce

570 ml (1 pt) milk

45 g (1½ oz) flour

45 g (1½ oz) butter

100 g (3½ oz) grated hard cheese

Method

Heat the oven to 180°C (350°F 160°C fan, gas mark 4). Put the potatoes in a large saucepan and pour over enough water to cover them. Bring to the boil then simmer until tender. When cooked, drain the potatoes and mash with half the butter.

Put the fish fillets, prawns and leeks in a deep oven dish and dot with the remaining butter. Place in the oven for 15 minutes.

While the fish cooks, make your cheese sauce. Melt the butter and stir in the flour, cooking for a minute or two over a low heat. Gradually add the milk, a little at a time, making sure the flour is absorbed each time. Once all the milk is added, bring to the boil and simmer for 5–6 minutes until the sauce has thickened. Stir in the cheese and let it melt.

Remove the fish from the oven and add a layer of fresh spinach, pour over the cheese sauce and cover with the mashed potato. Sprinkle with the grated cheese and return to the oven for 30 minutes until the potato has browned and the cheese has melted.

TOP TEN STORE-CUPBOARD STAPLES

Here are ten suggestions for things that you could keep to hand year-round, to add flavour and avoid a last-minute hectic dash to the shops.

1 Dried herbs and spices

2 Cornflour – to rescue runny sauces

3 Dried pasta (cook pasta, add a home-made tomato sauce – fried onion, garlic and a tin of tomatoes simmered down – some frozen vegetables and grated cheese for an instant one-pot oven meal)

4 Frozen vegetables (see point 3)

5 Cheese (see point 3)

6 Tinned tomatoes

7 Garlic

8 Oils: olive, sunflower, sesame

9 Long-life milk

10 Tinned fish – if you don't feel like cooking at all, tinned tuna, mackerel or sardines on toast is fast, simple and nutritious

ETHICAL EATING OUT

If you do decide to eat out – and who doesn't love having someone else do the cooking now and then? – you can still make a sustainable decision. Eat at a local restaurant and support a small business, and when you make your menu choices, ask if the meat and fish have been obtained from sustainable sources. With meat dishes, look for rare or native breeds, which need to meet high standards, choose fish that hasn't been overexploited, and seasonal vegetables. Also look into the surroundings of the restaurant itself before deciding to eat there: does it use low-energy cooking methods and LED lighting; does it recycle; what about plastic packaging and reusable straws? What does it do with its leftover food – can you take it home with you? Contact the restaurant directly to ask these questions before you make a booking.

MINDFUL EATING

Of course, it's not just the actual food that's part of mealtimes; it's also about *how* you eat. To really get the most from your meal, practise "mindful eating" – that is, paying complete attention to your meal: rather than eating as fast as possible, really use your senses. Make your meals visually attractive, then look at the colourful plate in front of you, chew every mouthful thoroughly, enjoy the taste, smell and texture of your food, and take a moment when you've finished to really appreciate your meal. Using your eyes, brain and stomach in combination will also give your body time to establish whether it's full. In one research study, 64 participants were served lunch in complete darkness. Half of them unknowingly received much larger portions and they ended up eating 36 per cent more food. Eating mindfully, therefore, means you may not actually need that dessert!

MAKE MEALTIMES MATTER

We all live hectic lives these days: skipping meals, grabbing a quick snack as we leave the house, eating at our desks. But whenever you have the chance, eat family dinners around a properly set table, rather than being hunched over trays in front of the TV. Leave your phone in another room; ask your parents, your siblings or your children about their days and really listen to what they say; play a silly card game after dinner; or continue the chat as you tidy up the kitchen. If there's one thing we find out as we go through life, it's that spending time with our families is precious – so use this time to enjoy it.

PART 3:

GETTING AWAY

Getting away gives us the chance to leave behind the humdrum of everyday life and escape our responsibilities for a while. But it can mean different things to different people: traditionally it may be losing ourselves in a book on a sunlounger next to the ocean; for some it's the opportunity for an adrenaline-filled adventure break; and others may want to soak up city sights, nightlife and culture. If you need inspiration for cheaper and more sustainable ideas for escaping the rat race, as well as some extra holiday-related tips, then look no further.

FUN-FILLED HOME-BASED HOLIDAYS

The most straightforward answer to a cost-effective break from the norm is to take a "staycation", whereby you stay local, or at least travel within the country where you live, and if you want to, you can even sleep in your own bed! There are a couple of ground rules though: forget the alarm clock, no checking work emails and have a small adventure each day. But what to do?

WARM-WEATHER STAYCATIONS

Pick your own

Seek out your nearest pick-your-own farm and fill a basket with beautiful fresh fruit. Enjoy it in the back garden or in a park in the sunshine with a glass of bubbly. You are on holiday, after all.

Bathe in sunlight

Head for woodland and spend the day "forest bathing". The Japanese call this *shinrin-yoku* and it means to be calm and quiet among the trees, while you observe and enjoy all that nature has to offer.

Become a local tourist

Look at where you live through the eyes of a visitor. Where would you go? If there's a museum you've never been to, a restaurant you want to try or a famous park you haven't got round to visiting, then now is the time. You could also head to your local information centre and ask for some recommendations – you might discover a hidden gem.

Spread some love

Why not host a festival-themed garden party? Get "festival-ready" by hanging bunting and lanterns and have friends and neighbours bring a blanket to sit on and some food to enjoy, while you provide the music.

Sleep under the stars

On a balmy night, borrow a tent and head out to sleep under the stars. If you don't have a garden, ask a friend if you can camp in theirs. Take your duvet along in case the mercury drops, though. Enjoy breakfast and fresh coffee in your own kitchen in the morning – as well as the use of your own bathroom!

Get active

You could use some of your staycation time to focus on a fitness challenge you've set yourself. Learn some more challenging yoga positions, do a "couch-to-5K" programme, practise your tennis game with a fellow "staycationer", or get in a few rounds of golf (mini or otherwise).

COLD-WEATHER STAYCATIONS

You don't always need sunshine and warm weather for a successful staycation; there are also lots of options for simple and fun cold-weather activities.

A movie marathon

Don your cosiest clothes, grab some snacks and a blanket and enjoy a movie marathon from the sofa over the course of a couple of days or a long weekend. You could even pick a theme: romcoms, 1980s or 90s teen classics, a complete saga back to back...

Bake!

Try out that detailed French patisserie recipe that you've never had time to make, bake a cake, make some bread. Fill your home with the warmth and aroma of freshly cooked food and then enjoy it with friends or family.

Wet 'n' windy walk

Chilly or wet weather shouldn't stop you from enjoying the fresh air. Wrap up cosy and warm, don some wellies and off you go. When you get home, have a warm bath then snuggle up on the sofa with a hot chocolate and a good book.

Find a new favourite

Visit your nearest high street and support your local businesses by checking out smaller shops you've not had time to investigate. You might find a fantastic local deli or a favourite new coffee hang-out.

Lend a hand

Do you have a local community centre or animal rescue that needs a helping pair of hands? They may be more in need of volunteers when the weather is colder. Giving up some of your own time to help others is a rewarding and humbling experience.

Old-school games

Head to the local charity shops and get hold of some good old-fashioned board games. Grab some snacks and drinks and invite a few friends over for a game night. Charades, anyone?

Have a scavenger hunt

Make a list of things to find around the house (e.g. a bar of soap, a can of soup, a dictionary) and send your kids (or your friends) on a scavenger hunt for them.

Write your bucket list

Grab a cuppa and a notebook and spend the day with your feet up by the fire. Make a list of all the things that you would love to do but haven't had the time for yet. Making space to jot these down on paper and really put some thought into them will give you loads of ideas for staycations to come!

BACK TO NATURE

Tempting adverts filled with sun-soaked beaches, sparkling oceans and exotic food can programme us to think that a "holiday" must be defined by getting on a plane. And while of course air travel is fast and convenient, it's often out of reach financially – not to mention the carbon footprint it leaves in its wake. So, while watching your finances may mean not heading abroad, it doesn't have to mean missing out. How about exploring the wonderful outdoor spaces close to home? You'll also be supporting the local economy – and no more stress-filled airports! It may mean a different spin on your break but a change is as good as a rest, no?

Camping

Sleeping under canvas is a fun way to get back to nature and relax, whether there's one of you, two of you, or a whole family. If you're a beginner camper, choose a campsite with top-notch facilities, rather than going full-on wild camping in the woods – you can build up to that. Lots of campgrounds have pitches with electricity, as well as pretty decent private bathrooms and shops on site – some even have Wi-Fi!

Glamping

If traditional camping sounds a little too daunting, then you could always opt for something slightly more luxurious and go glamping. You're still on a campsite sleeping under the stars but you'll stay in a comfortable and cosy wooden "pod" or a yurt, for example, on a proper bed with pillows. There are some stunning glamping locations, so take a look online for an opportunity to immerse yourself in the great outdoors.

Walking holidays

A walking holiday is the perfect way to take in the sights and absorb some of the best scenery where you are – as well as an opportunity to be "on the ground" and really engage with the community. From city walking tours to mountain treks, self-guided or with a group leader, there's stacks to choose from. The best idea is to book through a specialized walking-holiday travel company that can organize things like the route and accommodation, advise you on what to bring, and make sure the level of difficulty is right for you. You could conquer a personal fitness challenge or meet new friends, as well as forge memories to last a lifetime.

Cycling holidays

If you're a keen biker, a cycling holiday could provide ample opportunity to explore new terrain and spectacular landscapes. As with walking holidays, booking through a company that specializes in this type of break means that much of the planning and luggage transfers are taken care of, leaving you to enjoy the freedom of travelling on two wheels at your own pace. Travel either in small groups where a tour leader can share their local knowledge, or completely self-guided using maps provided by the company.

WORKING AWAY

If you're the type of person who needs to keep active on a break, and you like the idea of absorbing yourself in a different culture, then a working holiday could be ideal. Not as arduous as it sounds, this is a type of "cultural exchange" whereby you either earn a wage or volunteer for a cause, to live like a local and support a community. It's a potentially life-enhancing experience where you'll meet lots of interesting new people – and it could also help when looking for permanent work. Opportunities include:

- working as an au pair or nanny

- teaching a language; for example, teaching English to foreign students

- becoming a private tutor

- volunteering with education charities or animal sanctuaries

- working at a kids' summer camp

- being a sports instructor or coach

- working in the hospitality industry

- house-sitting

- building your skills with an internship

- construction work; for example, helping to build schools

- fruit harvesting

- bartending and restaurant work

If you are leaving your home country, to qualify for a working holiday you'll need a working visa, the requirements for which will depend on the country you are visiting. You'll usually have to be aged at least 18 and you'll often need to provide health documents and an education history. If you make a booking through a tour operator that offers working breaks, it can provide help and advice.

STAY OUTSIDE THE BOX!

Living more simply easily extends to your getaway. So, forget the expensive fancy hotel and opt for comfy and quirky accommodation a little off the beaten track.

Hire a campervan

With a little planning, there's plenty of adventure to be found when you take a trip in a campervan or motorhome. You'll be able to sightsee as you travel, too, if you and a partner take turns driving. Park up when the mood takes you and move on when you're ready. You usually book a campervan through a vehicle-hire company, who will ensure you have all the relevant paperwork you need and talk you through your requirements.

Home exchanges

Exchanging homes with another family is becoming really popular and can cut the cost of a holiday. Arrange a swap with a friend yourself, or via an established company that does thorough background checks for peace of mind. You'll usually need to take out a (relatively inexpensive) annual membership so they can put you in touch with like-minded swappers. You'll also need to inform your home-insurance provider. Bear in mind, too, that homes aren't usually visited before they are listed, so check photos carefully and ask lots of questions of the owners; sometimes, looking after a furry friend might also be part of the deal!

Hostels

Hostels are found all over the world and offer simple and comfortable accommodation, which won't wreck your wallet. You can bunk up with other travellers or pay a little extra for a private room or a cabin. Hostelling International (www.hihostels.com) has access to a network of youth-hostel associations around the globe, so this could be a good place to start.

Canal barges

What could be more relaxing than waking up in your own private floating hotel? While away the days up on deck with a good book and a glass of bubbly. Lazy days here we come...

Farms

If you're not afraid of the odd early wake-up call, stay on a working farm and really get back to nature. Accommodation can include self-contained, self-catering cottages, cabins, caravans, glamping pods or tents. Help out with the animals and become absorbed in the surroundings of country life.

Treehouses

Yes, that's right; your childhood dream of a treehouse can now be a reality! Indulge in peace and tranquillity among the treetops and wake up to the sound of the canopy coming to life with birdsong each day.

DAY TRIPPER

Leave at dawn; back for supper. Try these ideas for wallet-friendly mini-trips in a day.

Get up really early and head to the beach to watch the sunrise. Take a breakfast picnic hamper and wrap up warm...

... or head to the beach in the evening to witness the sunset. Have an early evening paddle before you head home.

Tour a local vineyard. Make sure you have a designated driver who won't be trying the samples.

Go on an open-top bus or tram tour around a local city and discover its history.

Take in a show. Last-minute discounted tickets for unfilled seats are sometimes available at the door right before a performance.

Round up some mates to share the cost and try an escape-room experience.

Make a document of your neighbourhood by taking photographs and compiling an online album.

Go for a hike along a local trail, enjoying a home-packed picnic on the way.

Have a go at geocaching. Download the free GPS app to your phone and try to find a few of the 3 million "caches" hidden around the globe. Just be sure to replace anything you take with another trinket for someone else to find.

VIRTUAL VOYAGE!

You can now venture pretty much anywhere in the world, with just a screen, a decent internet connection and a comfy chair. The ultimate in sustainable travel, virtual experiences have become increasingly popular over the last few years. While they might not be a permanent solution to all of the real-world alternatives, they may give you the chance to experience some of the places on your bucket list completely free of charge. For example, Machu Picchu (www.youvisit.com/tour/machupicchu) and the Great Wall of China (www.youvisit.com/tour/doilan) are just a couple of the destinations that you can visit, along with famous landmarks like the Statue of Liberty (www.nps.gov/hdp/exhibits/stli/stli_tour.html) and the Eiffel Tower (www.toureiffel.paris/en/news/recreation/virtual-tour-eiffel-tower).

(Note: URLs active at the time of writing.)

SUSTAINABLE TOURISM

With climate change continuing to have an impact on the natural environment, we all need to make some changes to protect the planet, and this includes being more sustainable in our travel choices.

- When it comes to places to stay, think about choosing an eco-friendly hostel or hotel that actively minimizes its impact on the natural environment.

- Look for ethical trips and tours; consider very carefully any that involve animal parks, or snorkelling, which can damage the environment if not undertaken with care.

- Air travel is fast and convenient, but there are other ways to travel. Use public transport, walk or cycle when you're at your destination, rather than using taxis.

- In the same way we can support local business at home, eat at local restaurants and shop at local markets.

- Just as you would at home, take your litter away with you. Leave no trace.

All aboard!

One eco-friendly alternative to travelling by plane is to choose a destination where you can make your journey by train, or sleeper train. For one person (per kilometre/0.6 mile travelled), an economy-class flight emits around 133 g (4½ oz) of CO_2, whereas travelling by rail, it drops to 41 g (1½ oz). If you really want to cut your carbon footprint, the type of train is also something to bear in mind: electric trains will of course produce fewer emissions than diesel. And while it may need a little more planning and take slightly longer to reach your destination, you can spend that time either asleep or enjoying the scenery.

STRESS-FREE TRAVEL

So, you've booked your holiday and you can't wait. Brilliant! But how do you get there – and back – with the minimum of stress? In a word: plan.

- It may sound like extra work, but by washing up, vacuuming and putting things away before you leave home, you know you're coming back to a clean and tidy house.

- Arrange for a friend to pop in with a pint of milk and a loaf of bread before you return, so you at least have something to eat when you get home.

- Put fresh bedding on your bed. If you're arriving back late at night, you can head up knowing it's ready to fall into!

- Organize someone to feed the cat or the goldfish, or water the plants.

- If you're travelling abroad, make sure you know where your passport is several days before you leave.

- If you're staying in self-catering accommodation, and it's an option, shop online and have your food delivered for when you arrive.

- If you have emails containing booking references, e-tickets or directions, save them as an image and keep them in a folder on your phone so you can find them easily.

- If you're going abroad and don't speak the language, install an app – for example, Google Translate – on your phone.

- Arrange travel insurance. Allow yourself time to shop around for the best deal.

- Always travel with a basic first-aid kit (plasters, antihistamine cream and paracetamol).

- If you're driving, don't set off at 10 a.m. when everyone else is on the road; leave early. It's worth the 5 a.m. wake-up call to not be sitting in traffic.

- Cancel the milk and the newspaper if you have these delivered.

- For peace of mind, consider installing a few smart plugs so that your lights come on for a couple of hours each day while you're away.

TRAVELLING LIGHT

There's a lot to think about when you're going away, so only taking the bare essentials with you on holiday is a sure-fire way to reduce the number of things in your head – as well as the strain on your arms when you're heaving your luggage up the stairs of your accommodation. Using a backpack rather than a suitcase, for example, means you have automatic limited space, so you need to think carefully about what's vital and what's not. (Fresh daily underwear = important; a different pair of shoes for each day = not so much.) Or you could begin with trying to fit all your packing into a smaller case and only size up if you really have to. Sometimes it's tempting to think you'll need a complete wardrobe change each day; you don't. And in the same vein, you could take a combined shampoo/conditioner, rather than separate bottles of each. Honestly, once you get to your destination, you'll be much more interested in making memories than in what you're wearing while you do so.

TOP TEN TIPS FOR PAIN-FREE PACKING

1 Write a list of clothing you think you'll need – now edit it! Also think about what else you ought to take – medicines, snacks for travel, activities for the kids, and so on.

2 A couple of weeks beforehand, wash clothing so it's ready to go, then hang it separately so you don't wear it again.

3 Pack at least a few days in advance so you can rethink anything if needed. Weather forecasts can often change last minute!

4 Stuff socks and belts inside your shoes; and pack shoes inside shower caps to stop soles marking your clothing.

5 Rolling clothing rather than folding it means it's less likely to crease. Who wants to iron on holiday?

6 Think layers: if you're going somewhere cold, lots of thinner garments will take up less space than bulky sweaters.

7 Decant toiletries into smaller travel bottles and pack them in a leak-proof bag.

8 If you're away for two weeks, pack for one week and wash it while you're away.

9 Write a note and leave somewhere you'll see it for any "remember to pack last-minute items" – like your toothbrush and toothpaste.

10 Always take some spare bags to keep dirty laundry separate from clean for the return journey.

PART 4:
STAYING
CONNECTED

Keeping a handle on your social life (online and real-life) takes work. The internet, email, social media and messaging apps have made it super-easy to find what we need in an instant, as well as interact quickly with others; but does this mean we've lost touch with what really matters? Sure, scrolling through Facebook, liking and commenting is easy – but forging real and lasting connections with people we want to spend time with, as well as making time for ourselves, is much more rewarding. This section provides some motivation for you to achieve this.

PRACTISE SAYING "NO"

We've all done it: we say yes to meeting up with someone, and then when the time rolls around, the lure of vegging in front of the TV in our joggers wins out and we cancel. There are probably people in your life who you love to hang out with and wouldn't dream of doing this to; then there are others that you perhaps feel more obliged to spend time with. Learning to say "no" to things you don't want to do is a life skill not to be underestimated – use it in a social capacity now, and it will be easier to turn down a plethora of other things in the future, such as piles of extra work or unpaid overtime! Your time is precious, so spend it with people who bring light to your life and the rest of it doing the things *you* want to do: if that's spending Friday night on the sofa with the cat, so be it.

JOMO

Choosing to stay in actually has its own term: JOMO (Joy of Missing Out – the antithesis of FOMO, Fear of Missing Out) is here to help you feel good about stepping back from exhausting and draining social interactions that you feel like you *should* be doing, in favour of reclaiming simple time alone. So, don't worry about what everyone else is up to; please yourself.

DECLUTTER YOUR DIGITAL LIFE

Email

In the same way that a house full of clutter can make it difficult to find things at home, if your inbox is clogged up, you might miss an important message. To avoid it becoming a massively onerous task, try these time-saving steps.

1   How many times do you subscribe to newsletters and never read them? Bookmark those that you do read, then unsubscribe from the rest. This will address the issue of new clutter gathering. Unsubscribe, too, from marketing emails, to avoid the temptation to buy things you don't need.

2   Set up folders to organize what you are likely to want to keep – for example, receipts for online orders, information from the kids' schools, personal correspondence and anything else that's relevant for you. Instead of marking emails as "unread" to come back to them, set up a "Read later" folder; just make sure you do read them.

3   Get to work deleting any emails that you don't
    need and filing the rest. Do this when you have
    time over the course of a few days or weeks
    – perhaps with a glass of wine in hand! Use
    the search function to find any emails you've
    unsubscribed from in point 1. and select/delete
    them all in one go. If they don't have a link to
    unsubscribe, you can mark them as spam, so
    they'll land in that folder next time.

4   Read and delete: every time an email arrives,
    once you've read it, if you don't need it then
    hit delete straight away.

5   To avoid becoming overwhelmed and distracted,
    turn off the email notifications on your phone.
    Instead, set times for yourself when you go in
    and check to stay in control.

Social channels

As well as streamlining your inbox, it could also be time to address your connections and friend lists on your social-media platforms. This means you'll only see news from people that you actually want to see news from. For example:

- How many of your social-media friends and followers do you actually speak to in real life? If you've not communicated directly with someone in the last six months, then remove them. If they miss you, they can always request to follow you again! The same goes for anyone who complains constantly; their negativity will only bring you down.

- If you do want to stay connected with someone but don't want to be bombarded with continual photos of their perfect life in your news feed, then either unfollow them, or use the "snooze" function to stop seeing their posts for 30 days.

- Are there any social-media channels you don't use as often as others? You could remove your profile from these completely.

- How many minutes are sucked from your day

by information you're not interested in? As with your email, turn off your social-media notifications. You don't need to know the very instant that Bob burned his toast.

- If you're messaged constantly by someone you don't want to keep in touch with (e.g. an ex who still holds a torch, an old work colleague who you didn't get on with), then block them.

Minimize your life online

After you've decluttered your social feeds, try cutting down the time you spend on them. Social media is great as a bit of fun, but it's too easy to become obsessed with it, which can be emotionally draining as well as time-consuming; it's much healthier to spend time with people face to face instead and free up time for more interesting endeavours! The Screen Time app on your phone is often used to keep control of your kids' time online, but if you're serious about cutting down, why not use it on your own devices? Or try putting your phone in another room while you're eating dinner and leave it downstairs when you go to bed. You could even employ an old-fashioned, beautiful paper diary instead of using the calendar on your phone.

PUT PEN TO PAPER

Before phones and emails, letter-writing was the main way of communication. For the person receiving the letter, there's something lovely about hearing the "plop" of an envelope landing on the doormat. Real thought goes into a handwritten letter – unlike an email, you can't keep going back and starting again – plus it's an opportunity to unplug and use beautiful stationery and a nice pen. Older (and some younger!) relatives do still appreciate a thank-you letter when they've sent a gift, too, rather than a hastily dashed-off email or text.

Keep writing

If you want to extend your love of writing, you could find a pen pal. This can be a rewarding and fun experience: as well as developing another potential long-term friendship, if you correspond with someone in another country, you'll learn about a different way of life or perhaps even start to learn a new language. There are lots of websites to assist you with your search. Some are free, and others charge a small monthly or annual fee to put you in touch with someone. Postcrossing (www.postcrossing.com), for example, allows you to exchange postcards with other people all over the world.

REASSESS YOUR FRIENDSHIPS

Reducing or eliminating worry will help enormously when aiming for a simpler life, and something that can cause needless personal stress is a toxic friendship. Some common "toxic friend" warning signs include:

- a lack of empathy

- they can't be trusted

- they gossip (if they do this with you, they are likely gossiping about you, too!)

- they're self-centred and constantly talk about themselves

- they're jealous of you

- they take advantage of your generosity

- they complain about everything

- they thrive on drama

- they are stubborn; it's their way, or not at all

Gradually cut down the time you spend with toxic friends and increase the time you spend with those who bring you joy and laughter.

LET IT GO

Not all friends will stay our friends forever, that's just a fact of life. Sometimes – whether through work, via our children, or university, for example – people only enter our world for a while when we have things in common, whereas other friendships will last a lifetime. If you find you're the one always making the effort to keep in touch, with nothing in return, then perhaps the friendship has simply run its course. It's nobody's fault; just appreciate the fact that you were both there for each other when you needed it and then move on with your lives. Who knows – one day your paths might cross again.

SOCIALIZING WITHOUT THE FRILLS

If you're looking for some ideas on how to keep your social life intact, but without a hefty price tag, you're in the right place. Socializing isn't about how much money you spend, or where you are; it's about the people you're spending time with. So, with that in mind, the following few pages contain some ideas on how to have fun, and inexpensive days and nights out (and in) with your friends.

Days and nights (out)

- Visit the pub during happy hour – or go alcohol-free for the evening!

- Look for voucher codes or coupons: restaurants often offer for kids to eat free, two-for-one main courses, or free drinks with a meal.

- Eat at home, then go out for dessert.

- Head to an open area away from city lights; take some snacks and a blanket and look for the constellations.

- Go on a night hike.

- Go for a bike ride.

- Take a picnic to the beach or the forest.

- Go for a walk in the country and have a good chat to put the world to rights.

- Visit a museum.

- Go to the funfair or an arcade.

- Head to the park or the coast and play rounders, Frisbee or volleyball.

- Go camping.

- Go on a neighbourhood litter-pick.

- Go to a flea market or have a rummage round a car-boot or garage sale.

- Take a road trip to a new town; enjoy the scenery.

- Set up and take part in a scavenger hunt.

Days and nights (in)

- ◆ Meet at a mate's house and order a takeaway.

- ◆ Have a pampering evening.

- ◆ Host a film night; everyone brings snacks.

- ◆ Organize a "pot-luck" meal with friends: each guest brings a dish.

- ◆ Have a board-game night; drinking forfeits are optional.

- ◆ Watch an online TED Talk and learn something new.

- ◆ Play video games.

- ◆ Start a book club, then meet up and share your thoughts – as well as some good company.

- As part of a declutter, hold a clothes-swapping party or a DVD exchange.

- Get baking and host your own afternoon tea; use your best crockery and dress up for the occasion!

- Find a dance or exercise class.

- Teach yourself and a friend to play chess.

- Take a look at sites such as www.meetup.com for a free online community event.

- Visit your local library.

- Have a decorating party; many hands make light work!

- Go on a tour of a local brewery.

- Search online for free webinars.

CHECK IN ON YOUR NEIGHBOURS

Not everybody lives their life online or has family nearby and for some people that could mean it might be several days before they see a friendly face. If you have people who live alone in your neighbourhood – elderly folk in particular – take some time to check in on them. If you don't know them well, rather than just randomly knocking on their door, pop a note through their letterbox explaining who you are and where you live, with your phone number so they can contact you. They might appreciate some help with walking their dog, or household jobs like mowing the lawn or a bit of shopping.

A SOCIABLE NEIGHBOURHOOD

There's no reason at all why you shouldn't make friends with your neighbours. Before you go barrelling up to everyone in your street, bear in mind that not everyone is interested in socializing, so try not to be offended! But if you're new to an area, or even if you've lived there for a while and don't really know anyone, introduce yourself via a short note. Organize a street summer barbecue in your garden, or a firework evening or Christmas get-together for those who are interested. It's an excellent excuse to eat, chat, drink and be merry.

INCREASE YOUR (REAL-LIFE) SOCIAL REACH

Our reliance on mobile devices for entertainment these days means that some of us are on the way to losing the old-fashioned art of conversation. It can be awkward to meet new people in real-life situations, but random chats in coffee shops and on public transport could lead to a regular catch-up with a familiar face. Not sure where to begin? Here are some ideas.

- If you're on a night out with friends, ask everyone to bring someone that the others don't know. Make it a condition of the evening that everyone talks to someone new.

- Sign up for an evening class. You'll naturally have something in common with everybody else already.

- If you regularly see someone in a coffee shop, try making eye contact and smiling at them – it might spark a conversation! Join a sports club. Get fit and make new friends at the same time.

- Volunteer at a local shelter or community group. Meet new people and give back, too.

- Look for a part-time evening job. As well as a little extra cash in your pocket, you'll meet different people.

- Join a local business networking group.

- Get involved in the Scouts or Guides, for example, as a leader, and be a role model for young people.

QUALITY OVER QUANTITY

Being a good friend isn't about accepting every social invitation going, or planning extravagant events. It's about being present, emotionally, for the people we care about. So lavish attention on your friends' well-being rather than on expensive gifts and flashy nights out. For example:

1 If someone close to you is having a tough time, let them vent. Just be there for them. They will more than likely return the favour when you need some support.

2 Surprise someone who's had a difficult week with a spur-of-the-moment takeaway coffee and cake from their favourite coffee hang-out.

3 If your housemate is up to the eyeballs studying or up against a work deadline, do their share of the chores that day to ease the pressure on them.

4 Be reliable. If you've made a date to spend time with someone who needs a shoulder to cry on, don't back out at the last minute.

5 Be honest. A friend will always appreciate your candour if they ask for your opinion on how to tackle a problem.

DEEPEN YOUR PERSONAL CONNECTIONS

When you interact with other people, are you paying all the attention that you could, or are you distracted with your phone notifications and the to-do list in your head? Really connecting with people on a human-to-human level takes a little more effort, but it's worth it. Not only will the other person feel valued, you will both get more from the relationship. For example, smiling and making eye contact when you're in conversation with someone shows that you are genuinely interested in what they're saying and instils a sense of trust. Keeping your phone in your pocket or your bag, rather than on the table in a coffee shop or restaurant, demonstrates your undivided attention. Body language also shows how we are listening and engaging with another person: turn toward them when they are speaking; nod when you're agreeing with them; don't gaze past them and out of the window. Becoming a better listener can take some practice: don't interject when someone is speaking and repeat things back to them to show you have taken the information on board and understand. Ask open questions to encourage people to share more. It's OK to share similar experiences with them to show empathy but try not to let the conversation become all about you!

COULD YOU GO "SMARTPHONE-FREE"?

It can be hard to fathom, but at one point in time, there was no internet, and there were no mobile phones, no social media (gasp!) and no messaging apps. People kept in touch via a chunky landline phone, wrote letters to each other and had face-to-face conversations. But some of us now are actually deciding to go old-school, as we discover that the ultimate way to really unplug is to give up our smartphone. People aren't cutting themselves off completely – many are keeping a computer connected to the internet and have phones that aren't smart on hand for emergencies – but the advantages of having no smartphone are quite thought-provoking:

- you'll get to talk to more people – and an old-fashioned phone is a great conversation starter

- cost savings – if you want to reduce your outgoings, monthly contracts and data plans can be expensive

- you'll probably sleep better – blue light emitted from smartphone screens disrupts your sleep as it fools the brain into thinking it's constantly daytime

- no interruptions from notifications – you can turn them off, but admit it, you're still tempted to look

- less consumer waste – an old mobile phone will probably last longer as you won't feel the need to have the latest version all the time

- to break away from the pull of social media at your fingertips – social-media apps are designed to be habit-forming so your mental health will thank you for it

- there's no temptation to check your work email in your downtime

- your attention span will likely increase, improving your focus on both activities and other people

ARE YOU ADDICTED?

Smartphone addiction is very real. It is particularly prevalent in young people, where it's been linked to poor mental health, anxiety, and even impact on educational achievement. One piece of research, for example, carried out an investigation into problematic smartphone use, focusing on 41 studies involving around 42,000 young people. It found that around one in four young people had issues relating to phone overuse. If you have children and young people in your house, encourage them to take part in other activities and instigate "phone-free" days or limit screen time on devices if you can. As well as keeping a check on young people's phone use (which if you're a parent can be easier said than done!), remember that they do follow your example. So, if you're glued to your phone for many hours of the day perhaps it's time to cut down.

Eight ways to cut down your phone use

1   Keep track of your screen time using the settings on your phone – you'll be surprised at how those minutes clock up! Apps and features like Screen Time (iPhone) and QualityTime (Android) are designed for this very purpose.

2   Use a digital camera so you're not dependent on your phone.

3   Invest in an alarm clock to wake you up.

4   Leave your phone downstairs or in another room at bedtime.

5   Impose a rule to not look at your phone until after breakfast and spend that time in the morning making plans for the day, listening to the radio, and chatting with your family.

6   Set a timer for once every hour. Check your notifications, then put it down. Gradually increase the time between checks.

7   Move distracting app icons (i.e. the ones you spend too much time on) to the second and third pages of your home screen.

8   If you're able through your settings, make the phone boring to look at by turning on greyscale.

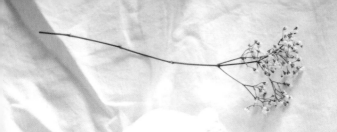

PART 5:
SELF-CARE

Most of us only realize it's time to look after ourselves when we begin to feel the effects of being overloaded, stressed out or under the weather; caught up in the everyday rush of life, we are often too busy to notice the signs of burnout. But it's vital to look after our mind and body *before* we get to this stage, to help us better cope with whatever life throws at us next. Self-care can feel like an indulgence, but it really shouldn't. How often do you actually truly relax and properly unwind? If the answer is not very often, then this section is for you.

CHECK IN WITH YOUR EMOTIONS

On a scale of 1 to 5, where 1 is "I feel rubbish" and 5 is "I feel fabulous", how are you feeling today? If you are hovering between 1 and 3 most days, then it could be time to introduce a little more self-care into your life. Now look at the following ten points and think about your answer – ☺ or ☹: be honest!

☺ / ☹   I know how to relax.

☺ / ☹   I exercise.

☺ / ☹   I go to bed when I'm tired.

☺ / ☹   I limit junk food.

☺ / ☹   I eat my five-a-day of fruit and vegetables.

☺ / ☹   I take regular breaks away from work.

☺ / ☹   I take some time, even just 10 minutes, for myself every day.

☺ / ☹   I have time for hobbies and interests.

☺ / ☹   I spend time with my friends regularly.

☺ / ☹   I enjoy my own company.

If you've answered mainly ☹, this could be why you're feeling more "rubbish" than "fabulous". Looking again at your ☹ answers, think about what small changes you could make to turn them into ☺. For example, if you feel as though you can't relax, then using some of the tips in this section may help; gentle exercise and strength work can be really simple to incorporate into your day without having to join the gym; and if you're completely worn out by 8 p.m. one evening, then it's perfectly acceptable to turn off the TV and go to bed. Some days we just need a little more TLC.

A SIMPLE A-Z
OF SELF-CARE

To set you on the path to fabulousness, the following several pages contain some thoughts and inspiration for some simple self-care activities, from A through to Z.

Accept help. Rather than a sign of weakness, it's actually a strength to ask for help when you need it. It shows that you're placing value on your mental health.

Breathe. When you're stressed, practise deep breathing. Breathe in deeply through your nose and exhale through your mouth. Do this ten times.

Chat to a friend. A problem shared is a problem halved; or quartered if you chat to three friends!

Dance like no one's watching. Who cares if you have no rhythm? Moving your body to music releases a rush of feel-good endorphins (happy chemicals)!

Eat well. Eating healthy and wholesome food means that you're taking care of your body and your brain. There are shedloads of ideas for healthy meals in the Mealtimes section of this book (see page 36).

Forgive. If you're holding any kind of grudge toward another person, then learn to let it go. It will be a weight off your shoulders.

Get outside. Interacting with nature in any way, shape or form is an excellent mood booster – and think of all the lovely fresh air filling your lungs.

Hobbies. Spending time doing things that you love is really helpful for your sense of well-being and calm. Simple activities like jigsaws, knitting or cross-stitch will give you a creative focus.

Invest in yourself. Is there a new skill you want to learn or a classic novel you'd love to read? Follow the tips in this book and make time to do it.

Jog in the sunshine. Even better, jog with a friend in the sunshine. Catch up on the gossip and exercise at the same time!

Kindness. Showing compassion and consideration to others will bring feelings of happiness – to you and to them.

Laugh! This is honestly the best medicine. Laugh loudly and often.

Me time. Making time for yourself is vital for self-care. And it's even OK to do absolutely nothing – see page 157.

Nutrients. We don't just get these from food. Getting out in the sunlight regularly, for example, ensures your body obtains enough vitamin D, which is vital for healthy bones and teeth, and supporting your immune system.

Organize. There are some great tips on home organization within "In the Home" at the start of this book (see page 6). Decluttering will bring peace and calm to your space, meaning that you'll feel less overloaded.

Pets. Animals bring contentment. Cuddle a cat or a rabbit, or take your dog for a walk. If you don't have a dog, borrow one from somebody else!

Quit. Whether it's smoking, eating junk food, watching too much TV... take stock of your bad habits, and try to replace them with things that will benefit you.

Reconnect. Sometimes life just gets in the way; if there's an old friend who you've lost touch with, reopen the lines of communication. Remember what you love about them.

Spend time with your thoughts. Take some time out each day to sit quietly and write down any plans, thoughts or ideas in a journal.

Take a tech break. Social-media obsession can make you feel drained and sap your self-esteem. Take the weekend off and spend it in the real world.

Understand your triggers. If certain people annoy you, or bring stress into your life, learn to recognize this. Perhaps try not to spend so much time with these people and rather concentrate on those who make you feel good.

Vision board. What are your larger goals in life for the next few months, or years? Create a vision board and use it as inspiration to keep your focus.

Work–life balance. This is absolutely essential for your self-care. It's not easy when you work at home, for example, to down tools and separate your job from your home life. Take regular breaks, too: the Swedish actually have a special word for a coffee and cake break (*fika*) to set aside a moment for quality time. (See also page 34, *lagom*.)

X marks the spot. If you live with other people, find somewhere in your home each day where you can switch off and unwind, away from the TV, the radio and everyone else. Ask your housemates or family to give you some space when you're there, even if it's only for 15 minutes of quiet meditation or a relaxing bubble bath.

Yoga. Find a 10- or 20-minute workout on YouTube and practise it each morning before work, or at the end of the day before you turn in for the night.

Zen. Follow all of the tips in this book to find yours!

FILTER OUT
THE NOISE

Have faith in yourself

Managing your self-care includes learning to trust your own judgement when it comes to your internal decision-making process. Your own gut instinct should never be underestimated. If something isn't right, then change it – whether that be ending a relationship, rehoming a pet or deciding to move house. You can bet that someone you know is going to have an opinion about it: that you've made a mistake, they would have done it differently, they know someone who could have offered some advice... you get the idea. "Armchair experts" are everywhere, but you alone are the one who matters; you decided to do this for a reason.

Avoid online advice

Armchair experts aren't limited to people you actually know; the internet is full of them! When you have a personal decision to make, try to steer clear of social media and websites full of information and stories about what other people did in your situation. Every one of us is unique and our "tipping point" for situations is never the same. Instead of spending hours online poring over what Sarah did when she was offered a job overseas, take some time out, go for a walk in the fresh air or make a list of pros and cons regarding the decision you're about to make. Filter out the cynics, be kind to yourself and do what is right for you.

THE SIMPLICITY
OF A ROUTINE

Humans are creatures of habit, so one of the ways that you could aim to reduce stress and bring a little order to your life is to set a daily routine. For example, if your job and family commitments allow, getting up and going to bed at the same time each day creates structure to your day, so you know exactly how much time you have available to get things done – meaning more focus and less time for procrastination. If you're an early bird, set your alarm for 5 a.m. to organize your day: make a to-do list, write in a journal, get some tasks out of the way, or just enjoy a bit of "me time" with some meditation or a gentle wake-up yoga session; if you're a night owl, flip that around and use the quiet time at the other end of the day. Allocating yourself plenty of time before work to exercise, eat a healthy meal or organize your jobs for the day means you'll be more motivated and better able to switch off when it's time to go home. If you're a "fly by the seat of your pants" person, then give a routine a try; your mental health will love you for it.

CHOOSE OPTIMISM

With all the bad news going on in the world at any time, it can be very tempting to get caught up in the doom and gloom of it all. But choosing to focus on positive news will do wonders for your state of mind and personal well-being. Mainstream news outlets can often focus on negative headlines, for example, as these are more likely to grab our attention – but for every terrible thing that's happening, there are some amazing and uplifting stories to be found, too. There are a lot of online channels and websites out there which focus only on good-news stories (type "I'd like some good news" into a search engine). And definitely stay away from reading online news before bed – "doomscrolling" (endlessly scrolling through news apps to read about bad news) is not the answer!

WHAT ARE YOU THANKFUL FOR?

It can be incredibly easy to take what we have for granted; 2020 taught us that. To that end, starting a "gratitude" journal can be a humbling way to remind yourself of all the things you are grateful for in your life. This could be anything pertinent to you and your circumstances, including friends, family and health, clean water when you turn on the tap, a roof over your head, your pets, food on the table or a regular job. Every evening, make a list of five things that you were thankful for today. Next time you're having a down day, use it to look back and reflect.

HALT

The HALT method began as a tool to help with recovery from addiction, and is now a recognized method for self-care. It can be used to bring you back to balance, and assist with anxiety and stress management. HALT stands for the four conditions of Hungry, Angry, Lonely and Tired. Regularly addressing all of these things in combination, whenever you feel them arise, can set you on the road to feeling more calm and more centred.

Are you **hungry**? We don't just mean the anticipation of a meal but rather the feeling that your body *needs* sustenance. Sometimes this can manifest itself as a craving for nutrient-packed fruit or vegetables, or perhaps your mind is wandering and you're having trouble concentrating on a task. Take action and top up.

Feeling **angry** is perfectly valid; we all get cross! But when feelings get out of control it's time to address them. Anger can reveal itself in numerous ways, such as being short-tempered or mean to someone for no reason. Learning how to deal with anger is different for all of us; some people need to pound it off on a treadmill, while others might plug into classical music. Find something that works for you and use it. If you find that you can't deal with feelings of anger yourself, please speak to a professional.

Being **lonely** can become an issue for anyone, of any age, whether you're a natural introvert or an exuberant extrovert. If you're comfortable in your own company, that's great; but no human contact at all isn't good for us in the long run. Even if it's a weekly virtual pub quiz, step out of your comfort zone sometimes to connect with other people.

Recognizing the fact that you're **tired** may sound very simple, but quite often we fight it – how can we possibly go to bed at the same time as the kids on a Friday night?! News flash: there are no prizes for staying up late. Burning the midnight oil too often will result in exhaustion.

ENJOY THE MOMENT

Do you ever find yourself clock-watching, wishing the day away? We all do it. Then at the end of the year, we wonder where the time has gone. One day, we will look back and realize that those small moments – our kids holding our hands on the walk to school, getting soaked in a downpour at a festival, family celebrations where everyone was together – are the things we will remember the most. If you have children, for example, they can come out with some spectacular phrases and nuggets of wisdom. So you don't forget them in years to come, jot them down on a piece of paper and keep them safe in a jar; they'll make great conversation starters at their 21st birthday party! Pay attention to the small things every day.

MAKE
SOMEONE SMILE

Another great way to live in the moment and be spontaneous is through random acts of kindness. Making someone's day will make yours, too. If you remembered to wear a coat with a hood on the school run, offer someone else your umbrella. Time left on your car-park ticket? Pass it to someone else. Let someone with only a few items through the checkout before you. Loads more ideas and inspiration can be found on the website of the Random Acts of Kindness Foundation (www.randomactsofkindness.org).

A few ideas for random acts of kindness

- Make dinner for someone who's going through a tough time and drop it round to them.

- Put your spare change in a charity collection tin.

- Offer your seat to someone on public transport.

- Leave biscuits out for the people who collect your bin.

- Babysit for someone so they can have a night out.

- Pay someone a compliment; it could make their day.

- Mow an elderly neighbour's lawn.

MOVE MORE

Keeping active can lower your risk of heart disease by 35 per cent, as exercising regularly means that your heart becomes fitter and stronger. Looking after your body will also take care of your mental health, as physical activity releases endorphins, which can reduce anxiety. Exercise doesn't mean pelting out a 5K every weekend, although you can if you want to! You can easily incorporate smaller things into your day to begin with to build your muscle tone and strength, and then work up to more.

◆ Practise balancing on one leg while you wait for the kettle to boil or the coffee to brew. Now can you do it with your eyes closed?

◆ Walk around at home on tiptoes sometimes, to strengthen your ankles and your calf muscles.

◆ Use cans of soup as weights and practise some bicep curls while you're listening in on a conference call or webinar, or simply take the call walking around rather than sitting at a desk.

- Dance to a disco playlist while you make dinner.

- Power-walk to buy milk at the local shop, rather than stroll.

- When you're at work, take the stairs instead of the escalator or the lift; if you work at home, walk up the stairs to use an upstairs bathroom rather than the downstairs loo.

- If you're in walking distance of a local shop, actually walk rather than drive. If you need to drive, then park your car a bit further away from the shop entrance.

- Weeding in the garden will give your whole body a good workout; it can be surprising how much you can feel this the next day!

SELF-CARE TIPS FOR HOME WORKERS

With many of us now working from home – either some or all of the time – self-care isn't confined to your downtime; it is just as important during working hours. But how do you schedule self-care into a working day?

One of the most important things to get to grips with is separating your work time from home time. This is especially tricky if you're sitting at the kitchen table. Set boundaries for yourself: start work at a certain time, and decide when work ends and your evening starts.

Always shower and dress, just as if you were commuting to an office, and eat a healthy breakfast. You don't have to wear your best suit – unless you want to – but you may not be at your most productive spending the day in your pyjamas.

If you begin work at 9 a.m., set a timer for, say, 11 a.m., 1 p.m. and 2.30 p.m. to force yourself to get up and move around. Make a cup of tea, grab a piece of fruit, or do some lunges round the kitchen! Keep only a half-full bottle of water on your desk, so that you have to get up to refill it.

GO TO BED!

Getting enough good-quality sleep is one of the best things we can do for our own self-care. There are three stages of sleep: 1 (light sleep/dozing off); 2 (when you start to drift away from the real world); and 3 (deep sleep, which restores and re-energizes us). It's important to make sure you get enough sleep to allow ample time for each stage – most adults need between 7 and 9 hours each night, and children and teens need even more. Getting plenty of shut-eye also keeps our immune system healthy, as well as balancing our appetites by regulating levels of the hormones that play a role in our feelings of hunger and fullness. When we're tired, we may eat more, leading to weight gain.

HOW TO REST WELL

◆ Sleep in a well-ventilated room. You'll generally sleep better when you're cooler. Decluttering your bedroom using some of the tips on page 12 will also help you to switch off.

◆ Set yourself a bedtime routine: put your phone away, read a book, have a bath, or do some quiet meditation to help you relax. Why not try the meditative breathing exercise on page 155?

◆ Avoid stimulants, like caffeine, or eating rich food within a few hours of bed. Alcohol may help you to fall asleep initially, but through the night it can disrupt your sleep patterns.

MEDITATION FOR BEGINNERS

Meditation originated in India and has been around for centuries; nobody can say for exactly how long, but what we do know is that it can introduce space and calm into a hectic and overloaded life. With a few simple techniques, some patience and a comfortable corner, you can learn how to still your mind and find peace and clarity. To start, try this simple breathing technique for 15 minutes to slow down and observe your breath as it moves around your body; either before bed or first thing in the morning is ideal, but you can do this at any time of the day. As you become more practised, you can increase your focus and count the number of breaths you take, increasing this number with each session. There are also some great guided meditation apps and online sessions if you'd like some assistance.

A BREATHING TECHNIQUE

Find somewhere quiet and comfy to sit. Make sure you're sitting straight, then close your eyes. Concentrate on the present; listen to the sounds around you. As any thoughts come into your head, let them pass through your mind, observing them as they go. Feel how your breath enters and moves around your body. Don't try and change it; just observe. Each time more thoughts arrive, again let them pass through, then bring your mind back to the present.

DON'T IGNORE A NIGGLE

Keeping in tune with your body is a vital element of taking care of yourself. Take time to notice how it moves, how it feels and what's normal for you. It's pretty common to get the odd sore muscle if we've overdone it with exercise, or to have a bit of a headache after overindulgence or a really late night – but if aches, pains and general feelings of malaise are happening more often than you think they should, seek some advice. And don't feel too bad if you swap a training session for an early night; it might just be what you need today. Our body is an amazing machine and it's very good at letting us know when something isn't quite right.

THE DUTCH GUIDE
TO *NIKSEN*

If you've ever had an "aha!" moment when you're in the shower or throwing socks into the washing machine, then you know that when we're not concentrating on anything in particular, our mind can get to work finding the solution to a problem or coming up with an idea. But us human beings can often be uncomfortable with consciously doing nothing; here, we should take some advice from the Dutch. The art of *niksen* is similar in some ways to mindfulness and means "to do nothing, without purpose" – so (quite literally) allow yourself to stare into the distance and simply let your mind wander. Who knows what could arise?

CONCLUSION

Well, there you have it. It may be the end of the book, but it's just the beginning of your simpler life. Through the tips and advice contained within, hopefully you've been inspired to make some small changes in different areas of your life to help you lead a calmer, more peaceful, and ultimately simpler and more sustainable existence. I wish you the very best of luck on your simple-living journey.

Image credits

Cover image – © AliceCam/ Shutterstock.com

p.5 – © suhyeon-choi-ehxwis6Ltxg-unsplash
pp.6–7 © Jafara/Shutterstock.com
p.11 – © Dmitry Galaganov/ Shutterstock.com
p.15 – © debby-hudson-VYS0KKGPEIU-unsplash
p.19 – © federica-galli—4qhiC6RmQw-unsplash
p.20 – © micheile-henderson-ZVprbBmT8QA-unsplash
p.25 – © jonathan-kemper-H488ymQglgM-unsplash
p.31 – © mike-marquez-082Z-3uTRAQ-unsplash.jpg
p.32 – © alyssa-strohman-TS—uNw-JqE-unsplash
p.35 – © Daria Minaeva/ Shutterstock.com
pp.36–7 – © ostap-senyuk—yow4azBP8k-unsplash
p.39 © Vincenzo De Bernardo/ Shutterstock.com
p.45 – © engin-akyurt-drzuouPgmoU-unsplash
p.46 – © david-becker-7hRx0xpTEhs-unsplash
p.49 – © Nina Firsova/ Shutterstock.com
p.55 – © Sea Wave/ Shutterstock.com
p.56 – © 5PH/Shutterstock.com
p.59 – © Martin Turzak/ Shutterstock.com
p.65 – ©bundo-kim-rXh4q1e-4Zw-unsplash
p.67 – © brooke-lark-nBtmglfYoHU-unsplash
pp.68–9 – © Olga Pink/ Shutterstock.com
p.71 – © kyle-thacker-leCSFQLc-Fs-unsplash
p.72 – © etienne-delorieux-oLbFi_xNi1c-unsplash
pp.74–5 – © Flaffy/ Shutterstock.com
p.76 – © Rasstock/Shutterstock.com

p.78 – © andrew-neel-a_K7R1kugUE-unsplash
p.79 – © denise-jans-1i4VSPPBy84-unsplash
pp.82–3 – © martin-kallur-ig-mkallur-l4m_o4aFOn8-unsplash
pp.84–5 – © sonia-cervantes-mQuuDjNXeH8-unsplash
p.89 – © ashim-d-silva-4RcFjVc8JLQ-unsplash
p.91 – © marko-mudrinic-EW04roNVHLg-unsplash
pp.94–5 – © Maria Savenko/ Shutterstock.com
pp.98–9 – © Carolyn-v-TilvuqNnT4Y-unsplash
p.101 – © cole-keister-SG4fPCsywj4-unsplash
p.103 – © marta-filipczyk-Wk0Uh8jpKS4-unsplash
pp.106–7 – © kamon_saejueng/ Shutterstock.com
p.109 – © mycteria/ Shutterstock.com
p.111 – © ethan-dow-TziAdI8DLJE-unsplash
pp.114–5 – © toa-heftiba-nrSzRUWqmol-unsplash
p.116 – © tomas-jasovsky-d5SZqLkplrY-unsplash
p.118 – © Charisse-kenion-w4VtT8jQL6A-unsplash
pp.120–1 – © Zephyr_p/ Shutterstock.com
pp.126–7 – © jen-p-FoG8lotg7AA-unsplash
p.133 – © conner-baker-F7m-YKqqBFQ-unsplash
pp.136–7 – © dedu-adrian-xEqeuD6J-Ls-unsplash
p.139 – © pure-julia-sx0VVRZpj6s-unsplash
p.141 – © prophsee-journals--jDNrq40idE-unsplash
pp.144–5 – © Natalya Lys/ Shutterstock.com
p.150 – © Floral Deco/ Shutterstock.com
p.152 – © graes-magazine-zDHUYnBdesl-unsplash
p.155 – © kenrick-mills-Wr7_0D6THK0-unsplash

If you're interested in finding out more about our books, find us on Facebook at **Summersdale Publishers**, on Twitter at @Summersdale and on Instagram at @Summersdalebooks.

www.summersdale.com